Game Changers

☺

Game Changers

50 Ways to Make Life Awesome

Vol. 1

By Justin Bilancieri

A Culture Craft book

CultureCraftCollective.com

Thank you dearly to my sister, Joanna Bilancieri for
the amazing editing you did on this book! You confirm
the adage that if you want something done, give it to a
busy person. Thank you for taking the time to edit this!

Thanks, Earth for allowing us to live on you. I know we can be a handful at times. This book is dedicated to making us less of a handful.

Have fun with this book! Read it front to back, or feel free to open it randomly and read one Game Changer at a time.

Life is about to get a
whole lot better..

Introduction

This book was written to share some of the wisdom that I, the author, have gathered along my journey. Everyone and anyone can benefit from this book. The bits of wisdom contained here are less commonly known ways to make life awesome. Having a healthy diet, getting regular exercise, and getting enough rest are probably the three biggest things we can do to live a long, healthy, and happy life. However, adding in the ingredients from this book will make it that much better. I invite you to dig in and start living an even more amazing life!

LAUGH

Lighten up and laugh.

Having a sense of humor is key to living
a less stressful, more engaging, easier
life with more fun. Make the effort to look
for humor in the world around you. It can
completely change your mindset which
ultimately changes the world. People are
attracted to laughter and those with a
sense of humor. Laughter makes life better
for everyone!

LOVE

Next time someone irks you to any degree, say to yourself "unconditional love".

Say it a few times. Say it over and over if necessary or until you feel the effect. Really sit with the feeling. It's truly game-changing. You end up laughing in place of feeling angry. Awesome!

PAIN

Let pain be the trigger.

Let any pain you may have trigger you to consciously send the pain love. Simply place love inside the pain, breath in and out of the pain, and see what happens. Keep placing more and more love there. Whether it's placing the word love inside the pain, feeling love in the pain, or giving the pain a good ol' rub and caring attention, this can surely be a game changer for all your aches and pains.

CENTER

Move from your center of balance.

In other words, all movement originates from your core, located a few inches below your navel. In Tai Chi, this is referred to as the tan tien. Soften your knees, relax your spine, and feel all movement originating from your core. This takes some practice, but over time it becomes automatic. This might up your dancing game, too! Bonus.

PLANTS

Try eating what comes from plants, at least most of the time.

There is a lot of debate on this topic. Don't be fooled, humans are biologically designed to consume plants. Compare our anatomy to the anatomy of the wild and it will be clear to you. Try it for 30 days and see how you feel. What do you have to lose besides a few extra pounds?

GARDEN

Make a garden and use it.

Getting your hands in the soil regularly has been proven time and time again to have many therapeutic effects. On top of all the wonderful health benefits you get from tilling soil, you get to reap the benefits of eating the food that you grow! Sign me up.

BREATH

Slow down your breathing.

Even if for only 3 deeps breaths, take time during the day to slow down your breathing. It helps to relieve anxiety, helps you to make better decisions, and brings you into more awareness of the moment—the best place to be.

STORY

Tell yourself a different story.

If you think you're bad at ping pong and keep telling yourself that, then guess what? You're going to be bad at ping pong! Start telling yourself you're good and over time you will have a much better chance of actually being good. This is the old "fake it 'til you make it" idea. This applies to any life stories. What stories do you tell yourself? Not sure? Start taking note. Game changer.

IMPRESSIONS

Impressions left now create the future.

Whether it's the story you tell yourself and your body, or the feelings you leave in the people you interact with, the impression you leave today create the world you live in tomorrow. Making good impressions today can set the stage for a bright tomorrow.

WOMB

Try to remember what it was like to be in the womb.

Go back in your memory and remember what it was like to be you at different ages. Remember how you felt about situations, what you thought about, and what your personality was like. Go back in your memory starting with recent years and slowly go back to when you were a child. Then try to remember what it was like to be in the womb. Then, try and remember what you were like before you entered the womb. This one is a trip!

NOTICE

Take notice of your thoughts.

This sounds easier than it is. So much of what we think about goes below our radar. Think about what you think about and analyze your thoughts. Let go of the stories you tell yourself that don't serve you and let go of any thoughts that don't serve a purpose in your life.

PEACE

Acknowledge the peace around you.

If your current space is not peaceful, move to a space that is. Removing yourself from situations that you aren't comfortable with is not running from the situations. It's being cognizant of your environment and how your environment is affecting you. You are in charge of choosing your own environments. The first place to start is your bedroom. Clean up your room. Make your bed after getting up. Clean out your closets. Clean under your bed. Once your room is a place of peace, you will always have a place of refuge.

LISTEN

Listen to others.

This is one of the most important life skills you can develop. Giving a chance for others to be heard is one of the most powerful things you can give. There are great quotes from best-selling books that go into this in detail. Oftentimes troubled people simply just want to get something off their chests. Be that person that gives them the opportunity. They and you will be glad you did!

IN

Listen in. Trust your gut.

It's true, you know best. You are constantly picking up information from your environment. Most of it lies undetected from your conscious brain. Listening to your gut, the second largest collection of neurons in your body, or using your intuition, takes practice and a certain level of trust. However, once you learn that your instincts can be trusted, you will never be left not knowing. Awesome!

OUTSIDE

Get outside for at least 3 minutes every day.

Getting outside everyday, even if only for a few minutes can certainly have an impact and be an evident game changer. Just having sky above you, even if it's a cloudy one, can lift your spirits and broaden your perspective.

QUIET

Quiet the mind from time to time.

Quieting the mind doesn't take much, but it can be difficult on the first try and even the second. However, like everything else, with practice, the easier it becomes. Simply stop the mind from thinking from time to time. Take a moment to recognize that you are thinking, then make the effort to not think. One common way to do this is by focusing solely on your breathing. When thoughts creep back in, go back to focusing on your breath. Simple, right?

REPEAT

In an anxious state, repeat 3 of your favorite positive words over and over.

Keep repeating them until the anxious state subsides. Maybe it's one word or a sentence, but have your go-to words, phrases, or sentences and be persistent with repeating them. Soon the anxiety and tension will dissipate. This gets easier and faster with practice, too.

FORGIVE

Remember, it's OK to forgive. Everyone. Even yourself.

Simpler said than done, but practice it and live more at peace with yourself and the world at large.

FAST

Try a 1-7 day fast at least once in your life.

Try a fast sooner rather than later. Put one on your calendar. Fasting can give you a whole new perspective on food and being hungry. Not to mention it gives the digestive system a much needed break. Upon research, you will find many health benefits can be incurred from a fast.

AWARENESS

Bring your awareness into your body while performing your daily routine.

A 3-second look inside your body for any discomfort can prove to be eye-opening. We often do habitual activities without any thought as to how our body is feeling while performing them. Take a look inside yourself and search for any areas of discomfort, unease, or tension, and then relax those areas. Soften the discomfort. Breath into it. Visualize breathing in and out of areas that hold tension. Then, go back to doing your activity with a new sense of peace.

FLUSH

Immediately upon awakening,
and just before falling asleep,
flush every cell of your body
with positive thoughts.

Make it a point to try this for 10 days and
see how you feel. Try saying the words
health, peace, love, strength, and other
positive words to your body. Feel the
feelings these words create in your body. Try
going through each body part individually.
This takes no more than several seconds
out of your day, but take as much time as
you'd like. Game changing!

SMILE

Practice smiling. It literally helps raise your mood.

Surprise someone today and smile at a stranger. It feels good, and it will make them feel good. The last time you got a random smile, how did it make you feel? Not only does a genuine smile uplift others, it sends feel good chemicals through the body, too. Those feel (you guessed it) good!

PERFECT

Understand that no one is perfect. Period.

It may be hard to do, especially when it comes to your parents, but keep this in mind while working through difficult obstacles in your relationships. It will prove beneficial!

EASY

Easy does it.

Take it easy. We've all heard it before and many of us say it on the regular. Well, it's great advice! Stress, as we all know, doesn't do us well. Sure, you can argue that a little bit of stress pushes us to act or gives us the motivation or strength to get things done, but overall stress is the big killer. No one is perfect. Not even you. Realizing this makes it easier to take it easy. You can relax now that the pressure of being perfect is gone. Time to take it easy!

READ

Read as much as you can.

Making the effort to read everyday has tremendous payoffs. It keeps the brain in shape, broadens one's perspective, and instills a sense of inner peace by expanding your knowledge. Not to mention it will make you an interesting person and ultimately a lot cooler. Shoot for reading from several sources everyday or try reading anywhere from a book a week to 3 books a day. Keep that up and you are bound for great mental shape! Your 'cocktail conversation' will leap from 'small talk' to brilliant dialog in the course of a week.

LEARN

Learn how to learn and keep learning.

You are a unique learner. Do you prefer reading books, hearing lectures, watching videos, experiencing things first hand, or a combination of these? There are four main types of learning styles: visual, audio, reading/writing, and kinesthetic. Knowing which type(s) you are will help you tremendously. Learning new things often, and keeping the mind active is one of the best practices for mental health long into old age.

BAREFOOT

Walk barefoot in nature.

Walking barefoot in nature is very grounding. Science suggests it dispels "dirty electricity" from the body that we pick up from being near so much electro-magnetism. It's also a way to connect at a deeper level with the planet that gives you life. Why not give it a try? You might even find yourself doing it regularly because it feels so good.

FUTURE SELF

Connect with your future self.

What does your ideal future self look like?
Out of the many possible future selves,
which one would you like to become? See
that self and go introduce yourself to her or
him. What does that person feel like? What
sort of things does she or he say? How does
she or he make you feel?

BODY TALK

Talk to your body.

Direct it. Let it know it's future. Visualize it in optimal health. Fake it 'til you make it if you have to. Making suggestions to your body will go a long way. Believe in this and you will see amazing results. Asking the body what it needs is a great start to recovery or optimal health. Ask away!

STEP

One step at a time.

As cliché as it sounds, it's some serious wisdom. One step at a time can apply to all situations. Not getting too far ahead of yourself, being present, and not moving too fast, are all applicable here.

FIRST

First things first.

Prioritization is key. Taking time for it will help you save time in the long run and will help keep workflows in order. Take a moment to strategize and find out what needs to get done first and then begin chipping away one step at a time. You may be asking yourself, "But what if everything needs to be done at the same time?" Remember. No one is perfect. Trust your gut, prioritize, breathe and proceed.

DO

Do to others what you'd like done to you.

It's the golden rule! It's been said many times in many places and rightly so. Ask yourself, "Would I like to be treated or talked to in the way I am treating or talking?" If not, others probably won't like it either!

KIND

Be kind. It goes far!

It doesn't take much energy or time, it can completely change someone's day, and it feels really good. Try it and you'll see. It might even open doors that otherwise would be shut to you. Think back to the last time someone was kind to you and remember how it made you feel. Don't ever recall a time when someone was kind to you? Well, try doing three acts of kindness today and see how quickly that kindness comes back to you.

GRATITUDE

Have an attitude of gratitude.

This goes far. It affects your mood, changes the vibe you give off, and creates better opportunities in life. With an attitude of gratitude, we appreciate the cup being half full, rather than seeing it as half empty. Like attracts like and this applies here. The more you appreciate, the more you are appreciated. The more you are appreciated, the more you'll smile. The more you smile, the happier you make the next stranger you meet. And, that stranger just might be the key to your next opportunity. Game Changer.

UNDERSTAND

Walk in others' shoes and seek first to understand.

Empathize. Really try to understand others' viewpoints and consider the events in their lives that may have led them to those viewpoints. Game changing for sure! Relationships will deepen, arguments will be easier to resolve, and you will definitely learn new perspective.

SUSPEND

As if suspended from the sky by a string, relax the pelvis, soften the knees, and elongate the spine.

Whether we are sitting, standing, or walking, practicing this quick visual is a GREAT way to put your body into proper alignment and to feel more at ease in your skin.

NAKED

Experience being naked in the wild. It's amazing.

Whether it's a skinny dip in an ocean or lake, a nude frolic in a forest, or a prance through a prairie in your birthday suit, getting out there and taking it all off is incredibly liberating. Do yourself a favor and try it soon!

NUDE

Sleep in the nude. It's better for your circulation.

You will find yourself waking up less throughout your slumber. It's also a lot more comfortable. At first this may feel awkward for some, but as you get used to it you will be so happy you tried it. Blood circulation in your arms won't get cut off as much. Turning over will be easier. And, you will subtly get more in touch with yourself. Try it. You'll see what I mean.

FORAGE

Learn how to forage in the wild.

It's not complicated and it will add a huge benefit to the rest of your life. Knowing which foods in the wild that can nourish you, will feel so good on many levels. There are great books on the subject. Find a local forager to get tips from or just watch what the deer eat.

ASK

Ask, believe, receive.

This applies to asking the universe, asking yourself, and asking others. You won't know until you ask. You will be happy you did. So, be brave. You have nothing to lose!

LET GO

Let go of who you think you ought to be and see whom you become.

Society, family, and our peers have such a huge influence on us. We often do and say what we think those influencers want of us. Take a moment and let go of your influencers' expectations and thoughts on what they think you should do, say, or be and simply see what comes.

BLISS

Follow your bliss.

If we listen in and do what makes us happy, at least most of the time, usually everything else falls into place. Believe it or not, you are meant to be happy. It's actually how you're wired. The impact this has on the world around you is incredible. It screams gratitude and respect. It's attractive. It also uplifts others. What an incredible service to the world you are doing simply by following your bliss. Give yourself permission today to follow it. It feels amazing!

HARD

Don't be too hard on yourself.

This can actually be a lot easier said than done, which may seem counter-intuitive. But, it is a big game changer when performed on the regular. No one's perfect; we know this by now. If you're doing your best then be happy with yourself. If you aren't doing your best, then start making the effort to do so. This isn't saying don't strive for excellence. It's simply saying go easy on yourself, and accept where you're at. Then go after more with the best of your abilities. There is always a next level to everything, sure, but do celebrate the small victories.

PERSISTENCE

Persistence pays off.

Not being too hard on yourself doesn't mean to not persist. After all, the squeaky wheel really does get heard. Don't quit. Take heed this advice. Be persistent in all facets of life. Things often take time to develop: Projects, relationships, skills, etc. Keep at them and before you know it, you will be where you want to be. Don't forget about taking a little bit of pride in your small victories along the way, and enjoy the ride.

PLORK

Play at work, work at play.

The idea of playing or making a good time at whatever it is you're doing is very powerful. We can find satisfaction and enjoyment in anything and everything we do with the right attitude. Working at your play is the idea of making your passions a priority in your life. Soon, they become your work and support you and you can call it 'plork'.

EFFORT

Life takes effort and it's OK if something is difficult.

Every great accomplishment in life has taken some level of effort. The greater the accomplishment, the greater the effort. Don't be fooled by the media bias that only hears about the success story. Dig a little into the history behind the success, and you will find years or decades of effort that led up to it. It's OK not to be a natural at something and still want to pursue it. Studies show that those without the natural knack often excel way beyond those with the natural abilities because they put in more effort.

PERSPECTIVE

Change your perspective and the whole world changes.

If you haven't ever experienced this before, it is incredibly eye-opening. Tomorrow, try waking up and saying to yourself, "I'm going to be in a good mood today." Make the effort to make this happen and see how the world responds. Game changer.

GRAVITY

Feel gravity upon your skin.

Take a moment to feel the gravity around you as it holds you on the Earth. Feel the light pressure on your skin. With this awareness, the energy around you becomes more apparent and that is useful for intuiting situations, removing yourself from situations that aren't serving you, and placing yourself in situations that do serve you. Take a moment now. Close your eyes and simply sense your body being held on the planet through gravity. Freakin' awesome and at no charge!

BETWEEN

Look at the space in between with a soft gaze.

Have you ever thought to look at the space in between physical objects? You may not believe what you start to see. Start by removing any visual focus. Then start to see throughout all peripherals. This is 180 degree vision. When you start focusing on objects, let yourself go back to the soft gaze. From there, begin to take note of the subtle energies that begin to appear. They can be fleeting, but keep holding the gaze and continue to notice what you see.

SERIOUSLY

Don't take yourself too seriously.

This is a very serious matter. The idea of not taking yourself too seriously is a major game changer. It lightens up all occasions and opens the door to a great perspective on life. Try it and you will not be let down!

MIRROR

Don't look in the mirror too much.

This may sound weird, but it's important. Looking in the mirror too much makes you nitpick yourself. If a hair is out of place, or you have a piece of food on your mouth, neither is a big deal. Each will work itself out. Relax, you look great!

BONUS Game Changer:

PREPARE

Prepare for the worst, expect the best.

When applied, this simple concept can relieve much stress and anxiety from your life. Knowing that you're prepared for all outcomes, you can then focus on the results you'd like to see. The saying "What you think about, you bring about" applies here. So, once you've prepared for everything, start focusing your attention on the best possible outcome.

Conclusion

The ideas in this book get easier with practice. Go at your own pace. You don't need to apply them all in order to have an awesome life, but do try and add the ones that resonate with you. I wish you all the health and happiness on your sacred journey through life!

About the Author

Justin Bilancieri resides in Boulder, Colorado. He is an avid singer/songwriter. He has published one other book to date called "TXT MSG Handbook, The Official Guide to Text Message Communication". When not playing music or writing books, he fills his time with photography, film-making, and exploring the outdoors. He only eats plants because he prefers not to fish, hunt, or otherwise harm animals. He believes that when we follow our passions, we live a long and fruitful life. Find out more about him on his website at www.JustinBilancieri.com

Also by Justin Bilancieri

The Official

TEXT MSG
HANDBOOK

VOL.1

A FULL-FLEDGED GUIDE TO
TEXT MESSAGE COMMUNICATION

Justin Bilancieri

www.ingramcontent.com/pod-product-compliance
Lightning Source LLC
Chambersburg PA
CBHW060039050426
42448CB00012B/3077